GCSE R NOTI ARTHUR CONAN DOYLE'S *THE SIGN OF FOUR* - Study guide (All chapters, page-by-page analysis)

by Joe Broadfoot

ISBN-13: 978-1516980000

ISBN-10: 151698000X

Brief Introduction

This book is aimed at GCSE students of English Literature who are studying Arthur Conan Doyle's *The Sign of Four*. The focus is on what examiners are looking for, especially since the changes to the curriculum in 2015, and here you will find each chapter covered in detail. I hope this will help you and be a valuable tool in your studies and revision.

Criteria for high marks

Make sure you use appropriate critical language (see glossary of literary terms at the back). You need your argument to be fluent, well-structured and coherent. Stay focused!

Analyse and explore the use of form, structure and the language. Explore how these aspects affect the meaning.

Make connections between texts and look at different interpretations. Explore their strengths and weaknesses. Don't forget to use supporting references to strengthen your argument.

Analyse and explore the context.

Best essay practice

Use PEE for your paragraphs: point/evidence/explain.

Other tips

Make your studies active!

Don't just sit there reading! Never forget to annotate, annotate and annotate!

All page references refer to the 2014 reprinted paperback edition of *The Sign of Four* published by Penguin English Library, London (ISBN: 978-0-141-39548-7).

The Sign of Four

AQA (New specification starting in 2015)

If you're studying for an AQA qualification in English Literature, there's a good chance your teachers will choose this text to study. There are good reasons for that: it's moralistic in that the text encourages us to think about right and wrong.

The Sign of Four is one of the texts listed on Paper 1, which needs to be completed in 1 hours 45 minutes. As well as knowing a nineteenth-century text from back-to-front, students will also be expected to know a Shakespearean play in full. More about that later.

Bear in mind, that you also need to be prepared for Paper 2, which consists of answering essay questions on a modern text, and on two poems categorised as 'Unseen Poetry' and two poems from the AQA anthology.

AQA have given students a choice of 12 set texts for the Modern Texts section of the exam paper. There are 6 plays: JB Priestley's *An Inspector Calls*, Willy Russell's

Blood Brothers, Alan Bennett's *The History Boys*, Dennis Kelly's *DNA*, Simon Stephens's script of *The Curious Incident of the Dog* in the *Night-Time*, and Shelagh Delaney's *A Taste of Honey*. Alternatively, students can chose to write on the following 6 novels: William Golding's *Lord of the Flies*, AQA's Anthology called *Telling Tales*, George Orwell's *Animal Farm*, Kazuo Ishiguro's *Never Let Me Go*, Meera Syal's *Anita and Me*, and Stephen Kelman's *Pigeon English*. Answering one essay question on one of the above is worth a total of 34 marks, which includes 4 for vocabulary, spelling, punctuation and grammar. In other words, this section is worth 21.25% of your total grade at GCSE.

AQA have produced a poetry anthology entitled *Poems, Past and Present*, which includes 30 poems. Rather than study all 30, students are to study one of the two clusters of 15, which concentrate on common themes. There are two themes which students can choose from: Love and relationships, or power and conflict. Within the chosen thematic cluster, students must study all 15 poems and be prepared to write on any of them. Answering this section is worth 18.75% of your total GCSE grade.

The 'unseen poetry' section is more demanding, in that students will not know what to expect. However, as long as they are prepared to comment and compare different poems in terms of their content, theme, structure and language, students should be ready for whatever the exam can throw at them. This section is worth 20% of your total grade at GCSE.

Paper 2 itself makes up 60% of your total grade or, in other words, 96 raw marks. Just under half of those marks, 44 to be exact (27.5% of 60%), can be gained from analysing how the writer uses language, form and structure to create effects. To get a high grade, it is necessary for students to use appropriate literary terms, like metaphors, similes and so on.

AO1 accounts for 36 marks of the total of 96 (22.5% of the 60% for Paper 2, to be exact). To score highly on AO1, students need to provide an informed personal response, using quotations to support their point of view.

AO3 is all about context and, like Paper 1, only 7.5% of the total mark is awarded for this knowledge (12 marks). Similarly, AO4 (which is about spelling, punctuation and grammar) only accounts for 2.5% of the total (4 marks).

Now let's go back to Paper 1. One of the difficulties with Paper 1 is the language. That can't be helped, bearing in mind that part A of the exam paper involves answering questions on Shakespeare, whereas part B is all about the 19th-century novel.

To further complicate things, the education system is in a state of flux: that means we have to be ready for constant change. Of course, everyone had got used to grades A,B and C meaning a pass. It was simple, it was straightforward and nearly everyone understood it. Please be prepared that from this day henceforward, the top grade will now be known as 9. A grade 4 will be a pass, and anything below that will be found and anything above it will be a pass. Hopefully, that's not too confusing for anyone!

Now onto the exam itself. As I said, Paper 1 consists of Shakespeare and the 19th-century novel. Like Paper 2, it is a written closed book exam (in other words you are not allowed to have the texts with you), which lasts one hour 45 minutes. You can score 64 marks, which amounts to 40% of your GCSE grade.

In section B, students will be expected to write in detail about an extract from the novel they have studied in class and then write about the novel as a whole. Just for the record, the choices of novel are the following: *The Strange Case of Dr Jekyll and Mr Hyde* by Robert Louis Stevenson, *A Christmas Carol* and *Great Expectations* by Charles Dickens, *Jane Eyre* by Charlotte Brontë, *Frankenstein* by Mary Shelley, *Pride and Prejudice* by Jane Austin, and *The Sign of Four* by Sir Arthur Conan Doyle.

Another important thing to consider is the fact that for section B of Paper 1, you will not be assessed on Assessment Objective 4 (AO4), which involves spelling, punctuation, grammar and vocabulary. This will be assessed on section A of Paper 1, which is about Shakespeare, and it will be worth 2.5% of your overall GCSE grade. In terms of raw marks, it is worth 4 out of 64. So for once, we need not concern ourselves with what is affectionately known as 'SPAG' too much on this part of Paper 1.

However, it is necessary to use the correct literary terminology wherever possible to make sure we maximise our marks on Assessment Objective2 (AO2).

AO2 tests how well we can analyse language form and structure. Additionally, we are expected to state the effect the writer tried to create and how it impacts on the reader.

This brings me onto Assessment Objective 1 (AO1), which involves you writing a personal response to the text. It is important that you use quotations to backup your points of view. Like AO2, AO1 is worth 15% of your GCSE on Paper 1.

Assessment Objective 3 (AO3) is worth half of that, but nevertheless it is important to comment on context to make sure you get as much of the 7.5% up for grabs as you can.

So just to make myself clear, there are 30 marks available in section B for your answer on the 19th-century novel. Breaking it down even further, you will get 12 marks maximum the backing up your personal opinion with quotations, an additional 12 marks for analysing the writer's choice of words for effect (not forgetting to use appropriate terminology - more on that see the glossary at the back of this book), and six marks for discussing context.

As you can see, we've got a lot to get through so without further ado let's get on with the actual text itself and possible exam questions.

Previous exam questions

Notwithstanding the governmental changes to the grading system, it is still good practice to go over previous exam papers. To make sure that you meet

AQA's learning objectives and get a high mark, make sure you go into the exam knowing something about the following:

- the plot

- the characters

- the theme

- selected quotations/details

- exam skills

Page-by-page analysis

Chapter One

The opening chapter is entitled 'The Science of Deduction', so clearly the focus is going to be on private investigator Sherlock Holmes's method of detection (1). We may feel surprised that he can detect anything, given that he is 'scarred with innumerable puncture-marks', which suggests he's an inveterate drug-user (1).

His 'companion', Dr Watson, who also narrates, takes Holmes to task for his bad habit. We discover that Watson is afraid of confronting Holmes, but does it anyway. However, the doctor needs 'Beaune' wine to fuel his courage, which suggests that he is a meek character generally (1).

Watson is also physically weak commodes to Holmes, as 'the Afghan campaign' of 1878-80 has taken its toll on him (2). Consequently, he cannot 'throw any extra strain upon' his 'constitution' (2).

We also discover that Watson is quite sentimental, at least in comparison to Holmes, who complains that his 'brochure' entitled 'A Study in Scarlet' is tinged 'with romanticism' (3). Holmes believes that the account should have been more about his 'unravelling' of 'curious analytical reasoning from effects to causes' (3). This suggests a huge ego and an obsession with science.

Holmes is very much a specialist and admits he has 'been guilty of several monographs', which indicate that he has been keeping busy writing in detail on subjects, such as: 'Upon the distinction between the Ashes of the Various Tobaccos' (4). Watson acknowledges his companion's 'genius for minutiae', which is an appropriate skill for a detective (5).

When he guesses that Watson has been to the post office, we discover how Holmes operates as a detective. Holmes reveals that if you 'eliminate all other factors' then 'the one that remains must be the truth' (6).

Nevertheless, Watson thinks he has stumped the detective, when he gives a watch as a test to see if Holmes can uncover anything about 'the character or habits of the late owner' (6). Much to Watson's chagrin, Holmes reveals that the previous owner was 'a man of untidy habits', who final took 'to drink' (7). Watson is upset because the previous owner was his late brother. For all his brilliance, Holmes realises he has been callous, saying: 'I had forgotten how personal and painful a thing it might be to you' (7). Although Holmes is a genius, he seems to struggle when it comes to conducting himself in a social situation.

This time, Holmes has worked out the truth through the application of 'the balance of probability' (8). There follows a detailed explanation of how he has put together a whole story through scraps of evidence.

However, he needs a greater challenge than the tests provided by Watson to keep him away from drugs. His stagnation is represented through the pathetic fallacy of 'the yellow fog' (9). The 'dun-coloured houses' show how bored he feels by his current jobless predicament (9).

Luckily, an adventure seems set to begin as his landlady, Mrs Hudson announces the arrival of 'Miss Mary Morstan' (9). The reader wonders what this alliteratively-named probable femme fatale could possibly want with Sherlock Holmes.

Chapter Two

In the second chapter, entitled 'The Statement of the Case', we quickly discover that Miss Morstan is quite exotic: her 'turban' suggests that she has some connection with India. The narrator thinks she may be far from well off, as the 'simplicity about her costume' suggests 'limited means' (10).

While she oozes vulnerability and 'intense inward agitation' with her trembling lip and quivering hand, Holmes is the opposite. The contrast is emphasised by the description of 'his clear-cut, hawk-like features' (11). This shows he is like a predator, while she is prey in comparison.

We find out that the date is some time in late 1888 and that her father 'was an officer in an Indian regiment', which explains the turban (11). Her 'unfortunate father' has gone missing and she needs Holmes to investigate his inexplicable disappearance (11).

There are no obvious clues in his luggage, and the only friend he has in England is 'Major Sholto' (12). To add to the mystery, Miss Morstan tells Holmes that she has received a 'very large lustrous pearl' every year since, on the advice of her employer, she published her address in answer to an advertisement (12).

She also shows Holmes a letter which, amongst other things, tells her that she is 'a wronged woman' who 'shall have justice' (13). She is told to meet the letter-writer outside the Lyceum

Theatre, but warned not to 'bring police' (13). However, she can 'bring two friends' (13). Luckily, Holmes and Watson are willing to take on the case and accompany her.

Although fascinated by the idea of solving the case, Holmes's lack of interest in people is evidenced by his comment that he 'did not observe' that Miss Morstan is 'attractive' (14). Watson is flabbergasted and calls Holmes 'an automaton - a calculating machine' (14). Once again, we see reason represented by Holmes opposed to Watson's 'emotional qualities' (14).

Holmes recommends that Watson read Winewood Reade's 'Martyrdom of Man', while he disappears for an hour (15). The intertextual reference suggests that Holmes is a social Darwinist, who believes in survival of the fittest rather than religion and sentimentality.

Watson, meanwhile, remains preoccupied with the 27-year-old Miss Morstan, who he describes as at a 'sweet age' (15). He recognizes that ideas of a romance with her are 'mere will-o'-the-whisps of the imagination' (15). He describes his future as 'black', which shows a deep pessimism on his part.

Chapter Three

The third chapter entitled 'In Quest of a Solution' begins at 5:30, when Holmes returns. He seems to think it's an open and shut case, saying: 'there is no great mystery in this matter (16). Sometimes, the renowned detective suffers from over-confidence, and this is an example of it.

The narrative uses Watson's obtuseness or comparatively slow understanding to tease out more information from Holmes in a form that is digestible for the reader. Holmes explains that he thinks 'Sholto's heir knows something [...] and desires to make compensation' (16). Watson is an excellent foil for Holmes, as he questions his companion by saying: 'It is too much to suppose that her father is still alive' (17).

The tension increases as Holmes takes 'his revolver from his drawer' (17). This suggests that he is taking the matter seriously with the expectation of violence. Miss Morstan 'pale' face adds to the impression that something dramatic is about to happen (17).

She shows Holmes a paper that was found in her father's desk, which reads: 'The sign of the four - Jonathan Small, Mahomet Singh, Abdullah Khan, Dost Akbar' (18). Holmes has to admit that he does 'not see how' it 'bears upon the matter', but nevertheless tells her to 'preserve it carefully' (18). Even if the characters do not know it, the reader is aware that it will be an important document as it echoes the title of the novel. The 'fog' that envelopes them emphasises the lack of clarity surrounding the case (18).

At the meeting place, 'a small, dark, brisk man in the dress of a coachman' accosts them, checking that the police are not with them (19). He whistles to a ragged street urchin (known as street Arabs at that time), who takes them to a four-wheel vehicle. Then they are whisked away. It is all so mysterious, as the utmost secrecy appears to be expected.

It appears that Watson has maintained his relationship with Miss Marston, as he remarks that: 'To this day she declares that I told her one moving anecdote as to how a musket looked into my tent' (20). He is relating his scary 'adventures in Afghanistan', but the 'broad, silent water' of the Thames, which they cross seems just as threatening (20).

They eventually reach 'a questionable and forbidding neighbourhood' in south London (20). Even the brick buildings are 'staring' (20). 'A Hindoo servant, clad in a yellow turban' opens the door (20). A 'high, piping voice from some inner room' is heard beckoning them in (20). The chapter ends on this cliffhanger as the reader wonders who the voice belongs to.

Chapter Four

There is a certain amount of horror in the scene that follows, as 'a blaze of yellow light' streams out, reminiscent of some similarly-colored scenes from Frankenstein (22).

Their host is 'a small man with 'a bald shining scalp which' shoots out of his 'bristle of red hair' 'like a mountain-peak from fir-trees' (22). His description relates directly to the title of the chapter: 'The Story of the Bald-headed Man' (22). We quickly get the idea that the host is mentally unstable as 'his features' are 'in a perpetual jerk' (22).

The 30-year-old describes his home as 'an oasis of art in the howling desert of South London' (22). By saying this, he displays considerable vanity. The reader must feel his portrayal is extremely unsympathetic.

He introduces himself as 'Thaddeus Sholto' and asks Doctor Watson to check his 'mitral valve' (23). Watson can only gauge that Thaddeus is 'in an ecstasy of fear', which is almost an oxymoron (23). The impression is that

Thaddeus virtually enjoys being afraid, as if he has masochist tendencies.

Thaddeus makes his brother sound like an intimidating person and he warns the group that 'nothing would annoy Brother Bartholomew more than any publicity' (23).

When Thaddeus blinks his 'weak, watery blue eyes' it reminds us of his lack of physical strength (24) However, the reader may distrust Thaddeus professed 'shrinking from all forms of rough materialism', given that he is surrounded by opulence and riches (24).

Watson suggests that they should set off immediately to Norwood to 'see Brother Bartholomew' given the later hour, but Thaddeus laughs 'until his ears' are 'quite red' (25). This shows that Thaddeus is quite contemptuous of other as he seems to look down condescendingly on Watson's quite sensible suggestion.

Thaddeus relates the story of his father, who admitted on his death bed that he had been afflicted by a 'cursed greed' that prevented him from sharing 'the treasure' with Miss Morstan. The reader may imagine that, like his father, Thaddeus may be guilty of 'avarice' (26).

Thaddeus's father claimed on his death bed that Captain Morstan had always had 'a weak heart', which makes the reader think there may be a family connection to Thaddeus and his 'mitral valve' (27, 23). It is claimed that the Captain 'sprung out of his chair' as they argued over 'the treasure' and fell cutting his head (27). Thaddeus's father kept the subsequent death secret for fear of being accused of murder.

Just when Thaddeus's father was about to tell his sons where the treasure was hidden, 'a bearded, hairy face, with cruel eyes' was seen peering through the window (28). Initially, the only evidence the twins can find is 'a single foot-mark' in 'the flower bed' (28). Later, 'a torn piece of paper with the words "The sign of the four" scrawled across it' was found' (28, 29).

Like a stereotypical Victorian female, Miss Morstan is 'about to faint', after hearing this account (29). By contrast, the heroic Holmes is leaning back 'with an abstracted expression' (29). Holmes is clearly fascinated by the case, as his eyes are described as 'glittering' (29).

Thaddeus, meanwhile, speaks in French, which translated means: 'Bad taste leads to crime' (30). It reminds the reader that his 'oasis' may be considered by some to be in bad taste.

Perhaps this is a clue leading us to the real criminal, which we may suspect is Thaddeus.

As they prepare to go out, 'no part of' Thaddeus is 'visible save his mobile and peaky face' (31). This indicates that metaphorically he may be hiding the truth. There is nothing honest nor wholesome about his presentation. The idea that he is a 'hyperchondriac' is repeated throughout the chapter, making the reader distrust him (32).

Thaddeus has taken over the narrative for much of this chapter, and this is further embedded by the use of his father as narrator. As in 'Frankenstein', the writer uses embedded narratives to add tension and mystery to the plot.

Chapter Five

The chapter is entitled: 'The Tragedy of Pondicherry Lodge' and, by 11pm, they reach the place mentioned (33). The title warns us to expect something awful and this is further foreshadowed by 'half a moon peeping' through 'heavy clouds' (33). This seems the perfect setting for some unspeakable gothic crime.

The building is 'vast' and, with 'its gloom and its deadly silence', it strikes 'a chill to the heart' (34). Bartholomew's window is 'where the moonlight strikes', highlighting a possible place where something heinous has been committed (34). Using the sound imagery of the housekeeper, Mrs Bernstein, 'whimpering', the narrator conveys to the that something awful has indeed happened (34).

Meanwhile, the horror of the situation draws Miss Morstan closer to Watson, as he discovers 'her hand' in his (34). He thinks it is 'instinct' that has made her 'turn' to him 'for comfort' (35). Unlike Holmes, he is forever looking for emotional explanations for behaviour.

Holmes remains in control of the situation and never lets his emotions get the better of him. While Thaddeus's teeth are 'chattering', Holmes is looking for evidence with 'his lens' (37). Watson assists Thaddeus, whose knees are 'trembling', but Holmes is only focused on solving the case (37).

'Moonlight' illuminates the death scene, as we see the grisly smiling face of a recently deceased Batholomew through the keyhole (38). This method of viewing the scene makes it all the more mysterious, as Holmes and Watson can only see part of the room until they break the door down.

Once inside, they can see 'a peculiar instrument - a brown, close-grained stick, with a stone head like a hammer, rudely lashed on with coarse twine' (39). At this stage, it is difficult to imagine exactly how this implement was used in the murder, but the reader trusts that Holmes will work out how it fits into the crime scene. Unsurprisingly, a note with 'the sign of the four' written on it is read there. Less predictably, the dead man has 'what looked like a long dark thorn stuck in his skin just above the war' (39). Holmes informs Watson that the thorn is 'poisoned' (39).

Then Thaddeus's cries out that: 'The treasure is gone!' (39). He claims he left Bartholomew at 'ten o'clock' and that now the police will blame him for the murder as he was the last one to see him (40). Strangely, Holmes reassures Thaddeus, telling him: 'You have no reason for fear, Mr Sholto' (40). This is uncharacteristic of Holmes, as earlier in the novel he tells Watson that 'a client is a [...] mere unit, a factor in a problem' (40). Suddenly, he seems less like the automaton that Watson accused him of being, and more like a human being.

Chapter Six

We learn a little more about Holmes's character at the beginning of this chapter, entitled

'Sherlock Holmes Gives a Demonstration' (41). He displays a superior attitude when telling Watson to 'just sit in the corner' (41). While he clearly values Watson's companionship, he doesn't treat him like an equal.

The narrative switches to the present tense, adding tension, as Holmes explains that the 'wooden-legged' suspect was aided by an 'ally' (42). He tells Watson that 'this ally breaks fresh ground in the annals of crime in this country' (42). By contrast, Holmes uses the past tense to describe the one-legged suspect, which makes him sound less dangerous as the threat is less immediate.

He continues to talk to Watson, as a teacher would to a pupil, saying: 'How often have I said to you that when you have eliminated the impossible, whatever remains, however improbable, must be the truth?' (43). Through the use of this rhetorical question, Holmes mildly scolds Watson.

The narrator compares Holmes to a bird, with his 'long thin nose' and his 'beady eyes gleaming' (44). Perhaps it refers to the detective's ability to pick the wheat from the chaff: an essential gift when choosing which clues to follow-up. Holmes has to be careful not to spend time on red herrings, or irrelevant clues.

Watson is useful to him, though, to confirm what he believes. Holmes uses him as a sounding board. For instance, when he asks his 'conclusion' as to the cause of Bartholomew's death (45). Watson replies that it was caused by 'some vegetable alkaloid' (45). He adds it was from 'some strychnine-like substance which would produce tetanus' (45). Holmes said that occurred to him 'the instant' he 'saw the drawn muscles of the face' (45). Once again, Holmes retains the upper hand in his dealings with his companion.

The next character we are introduced to is a police detective called Athelney Jones. He is described as a 'very stout, portly man in a grey suit' and seems to be the opposite of Holmes (46). Jones repeats himself, by saying: 'Here's a business' and then by saying: 'Here's a pretty business' (46). His method of detection is 'common sense', so he is worlds apart from Holmes, who is much more scientific in his approach (46).

Holmes is clearly more sophisticated than the 'fat detective' as, like Thaddeus, he can speak French (47). The translation of Holmes's French phrase is: 'There are no fools so troublesome as those that have some wit'. Holmes is quoting Francois de la Rochefoucauld, a French nobleman, with whom he shares the view that human conduct should neither be condemned nor celebrated. However, Holmes is observing that Jones is an idiot, who is not completely devoid of intelligence and that makes him a nuisance at times.

Jones refers to Holmes dismissively as 'Mr Theorist', when the latter reassures Thaddeus that he will be able to 'clear' him 'of the charge' of murder (48). It is obvious from this comment that Jones thinks of himself as more practical than Holmes. Nevertheless, Holmes tells Jones the identity of one of the suspected one-legged man: 'Jonathan Small' (48).

Holmes has no confidence in Jones's ability to find the real murderer, as he suggests leaving him 'to exult over any mare's nest which he may choose to construct' (49). The 'mare's nest' expression refers to someone's ability to discover something seemingly amazing, which doesn't actually exist. However, Holmes does believe in old Sherman's dog, Toby, so sends Watson off to bring back the 'queer mongrel' (49).

Before Watson heads off, Holmes quotes the 'pithy' German philosopher Goethe. The translation is: 'We are used to seeing that Man despises what he never comprehends' (50). It clearly refers to Jones, wrongly accusing Thaddeus, perhaps because of his exotic appearance which defies understanding.

Chapter Seven

This chapter is entitled: 'The Episode of the Barrel', so we can expect this object to be instrumental, at least in this part of the story (51).

However, it begins with Watson revealing his reluctance to take advantage of Miss Morstan's 'weeping' (51). He says it was 'the effort of self-restraint' which held him back. He seems a perfect gentleman, an excellent foil for a stereotypical Victorian woman.

When he leaves Miss Morstan with her employer, Mrs Cecil Forrester, he describes the pair as 'two graceful, clinging figures' illuminated by 'the hall-light shining through stained glass' (52). It shows the pair in a holy light suggesting purity.

Then we meet Mr Sherman, who is described as 'a lanky, lean old man with stooping shoulders, a stringy neck, and blue-tinted glasses' (53). Reading between the lines we can guess that he is hard-working, which has the 'stooping shoulders', but mildly eccentric, judging by the blue lenses.

Holmes, meanwhile, makes it clear that he is on Thaddeus's side, as he calls him 'friend' (54). He is clearly disgusted with Jones's arrests of Thaddeus, 'the gatekeeper, the housekeeper, and the Indian servant' (54). Taking the police sergeant's 'bull's eye', or small lantern, Holmes tries to get to the bottom of the mystery (54).

He asks Watson to 'loose the dog, and look out for Blondin', referring to the nineteenth-century escapologist, who was a famous tightrope walker (55). Adding to Holmes's magical aura is Watson comment that he's 'like an enormous glow-worm (55).

The dog is also revered for his ability to sniff out a criminal. Watson says that he's 'like a connoisseur sniffling the bouquet of a famous vintage' (56).

The setting the dog leads them to is incredibly depressing, 'with its scattered dirt-heaps and ill-grown shrubs', which have 'a blighted, ill-omened look' (57). All is decay, which is a common theme of turn of the century literature.

Holmes reveals that 'Jonathan Small did not get the treasure because he and his associates were themselves convicts' (58). He explains that Major Sholto was 'happy in the possession of the treasure' until he received a letter 'to say that the men whom he had wronged' were no longer in prison (58). Holmes arrogantly says that 'it is the only hypothesis which covers all the facts' (58).

He goes on to explain how Small wanted to regain 'his rights' to the treasure and get 'revenge on the man who had wronged him' (59). He left the 'sign' to show the act of murder was 'something in the nature of an act of justice' (59).

He believes that Small was aided by the 'butler, Lal Rao' (59). He adds that Mrs Bernsteing gives Rao 'far from a good character' (59). This seems strangely unscientific of Holmes, who is not usually prone to jumping to conclusions.

Indeed, he is more of a philosopher, proved when he asks Watson if he is 'well up' in his studies of 'Jean Paul' Richter (60). Holmes goes on to cite Richter's idea that 'the chief proof of man's real greatness lies in his perception of his own smallness' (61). This suggests that egotism has no place for the truly great people of this world, but in Holmes's case concerns his considerable eye for detail.

Eventually, Toby the dog leads them to a 'barrel', which causes the narrator and Holmes to 'burst simultaneously into an uncontrollable fit of laughter' (62). On the surface, it seems that the intervention of the dog has yielded no results, at this stage. The reader wonder what exactly this means, so the chapter is ended on a cliffhanger of sorts.

Chapter Eight

It is almost as if the dog is Holmes's gothic double, as Watson notes: 'Toby has lost his character for infallibility' (63). By trusting the dog's instincts, Holmes has taken Watson on a wild goose chase. However, Holmes will not give up.

He has a huge ego, which means he underestimates others. This is proven when he says: 'These fellows are sharper than I expected' (64).

As the pair follow the dog chasing a different scent trail to the river, they encounter Mrs Smith and her son, Jack. From her, they discover that the 'wooden-legged man' is a 'monkey-faced chap' with a 'voice, which is kind o' thick and foggy' (65). This description associates this criminal with mysterious weather, where nothing is clear.

Holmes explains that to get information from 'people of that sort' you must 'never let them' know that what they've said is valuable to you, or they 'will instantly shut up like an oyster' (66). This simile conveys the idea that the Smiths are a seafaring family. Additionally, we become aware of Holmes condescending attitude to the lower classes, when he says 'people of that sort'.

He displays the same attitude in his dealings with 'The Baker Street Irregulars', who the chapter is named after. He describes Wiggins, the leader of the group as his 'dirty little lieutenant' (67).

Meanwhile, Watson explains his dilemma. Being a moral man, he chooses to follow the righteous path of trying to deliver 'the treasure' to Miss Morstan, although he admits that if he finds it, it will 'probably put her forever beyond' his reach (68). He believes that as a rich heiress, she will be inundated with suitors and he will have no chance of winning her love.

We then meet 'the ragged little street Arabs', who are the aforementioned 'unofficial' child police force of Baker Street 'irregulars'. Wiggins is described as 'a disreputable little scarecrow' by the narrator. This makes it clear that Watson has little regard for Holmes's young allies.

After the irregulars are sent on their mission to 'find the whereabouts of a steam launch called "Aurora"', Holmes begins explaining who is responsible for the 'diminutive foot-marks' at the scene of the crime (70, 71). He says that a 'savage' from the 'Andaman Islands' must have fired the dart from 'a blow pipe' into Bartholomew's neck (71). The word 'savage' is offensive to modern readers, due to the inherent racism implied. However, during Victorian times, many readers would have not thought the term to be derisory.

Holmes reads to Watson from his latest 'gazetteer', which shows he is quite erudite and well-informed for his time (71). He quotes the book to inform Watson that: 'The aborigines of the Andaman Islands may perhaps claim the distinction of being the smallest race upon this earth' (72).

After all this mental work, Holmes takes 'up his violin' (72). This proves he is a genius in more than one field, as in music also he shows 'a remarkable gift for improvisation' (73).

Chapter Nine

We see Holmes's commitment to a lifelong education again, as he is 'deep in a book', when Watson awakes at the start of the chapter entitled: 'A Break in the Chain' (74).

Watson is shocked by Holmes's sexist misogyny, as he warns his friend that 'women are never to be entirely trusted' (74). Watson calls it an 'atrocious sentiment', emphasizes their difference of opinion on the fairer sex.

Although he is instructed not to reveal too much to Miss Morstan and Mrs Forrester, the latter's comment that the story of Bartholomew's death is 'a romance' suggests he may have given them quite a detailed account (75). Both ladies know that the story includes 'an injured lady, half a million in treasure, a black cannibal, and a wooden-legged ruffian' (75).

Miss Mary Morstan shows 'no sign of elation at the prospect' of becoming rich (75). This shows how virtuous she is, as Watson notes.

Meanwhile, Holmes shows an obsessive side to his character, as he is portrayed walking up and down rather than sleeping at night. As he readily admits, the 'infernal problem is consuming' him (76).

Possibly to take his mind off the case, Holmes busies himself with what Watson calls a 'malodorous chemical experiment' (77). The reader may suspect that this activity has something to do with solving the case.

Later, Holmes changes into 'a rude sailor dress' to go 'down the river' (77). He instructs Watson to 'remain' as his 'representative', as he expects news at any moment (77).

It is clear that Holmes trusts Watson, as he also instructs him 'to act on' his 'own judgement if any news should come' (78). However, nothing initially materialises except a report in the newspaper, revealing that Thaddeus and the housekeeper have been released without charge by the police.

Watson also notes how 'ingenious' Holmes is to put an advertisement in the same paper, asking for information about 'the whereabouts of [...] Mordecai Smith and the launch "Aurora"' (79). By saying that the information is being requested by Mrs Smith, Watson believes that Holmes is disguising the fact that it is he who actual seeks her husband and the boat. However, perhaps some criminals may recognise Holmes's address: '221B, Baker Street, which is also in the advertisement.

A 'downcast' Jones arrives at Baker Street, looking for Holmes, whom he describes as 'a wonderful man' (80). However, the policemen takes 'satisfaction' from the fact that Holmes 'has been at fault too' (81). This suggests a deep rivalry between the two men.

When Holmes turns up in disguise, both Jones and Watson are fooled by his 'aged' appearance, until his normal 'voice' breaks in 'upon' them (81, 82). Jones commends Holmes's impression of a 'workhouse cough', alluding to the miserable conditions endured by the poverty-stricken during the Victorian era (83).

It seems that Holmes is a man of many talents, as he vows to impress Jones and Watson with his 'merits as a housekeeper' (84). This suggests Holmes's extreme versatility and confidence.

Chapter Ten

We find out in alliterative terms that the trio's 'meal' is a 'merry one' (85). The repeating 'm' sound suggests music and enjoyment, a radical departure from Holmes's 'black depression' earlier (85).

Holmes reveals that he did indeed plunge himself into 'a chemical analysis' to take his mind off the case (86). This enabled him to consider Small's 'delicate finesse', which he claims 'is usually a product of higher education' (86). His admiration for Small's 'cunning' is clearly growing (86).

Holmes explains that Small would be unlikely to set off immediately in the 'Aurora', as his 'lair would be too valuable' to give up 'until he was sure that he could do without it' (87). The name of the boat foreshadows the idea that there might be a lot of light illuminating the darkness later, like the Northern Lights that it is named after.

While he was in disguise, Holmes reveals that he encountered the boat's owner, Mordecai Smith. Holmes seems to have little regard for him as he describes him as 'the worse for liquor' (88). The detective clearly thinks that Mordecai is like other men of his class, prone to 'chucking shillings about' when he feels 'flush of money' (88). This working class man is being portrayed as a foolish character, who spends his ill-gotten gains on alcohol.

We get the idea that Holmes is a gambler, from his comment that 'it is a hundred to one' that Smith knows where Small and the Islander are

(89). Holmes is quite exact with his odds, as he claims that it is 'ten to one that they go downstream' (89). From this we get the impression that Holmes is very calculating and mathematical in his approach to solving mysteries.

This is further emphasised by his insistence that 'you can say with precision what an average number [of people] will be up to', although he admits that 'individuals vary' (90). He has taken on the above theory from his study of Winwood Reade, an author he recommended to Watson earlier.

As the trio and their helpers start their pursuit of the 'Aurora', the pace of the narrative picks up, with the characters beginning to use shorter sentences mixed with imperatives like: 'Full speed ahead, engineer' (90).

Before long 'the dull blur in front of' them turns into 'the dainty "Aurora" (91). This shows literally how the mystery is slowly unravelling as the criminals come into view.

The Islander is unflatteringly described as 'a little black man [...] with a great, misshapen head and a shock of tangled, dishevelled hair' (92). The term 'unhallowed dwarf' makes the Islander appear diabolical, while his 'strong yellow teeth gnashing' suggest he is no more than an animal (92). By dehumanizing the Islander, the writer ensures that the reader has little or no sympathy for him.

The chapter is entitled: 'The End of the Islander', so it is no real surprise when he is shot and falls 'into the stream' (93). Even then, the narrator comments on the Islander's 'venomous, menacing eyes' (94). The reader may wonder whether or not the Islander is actually dead as there is 'no sign' of him thereafter.

Meanwhile, Small gets stuck in the mud-bank and is hauled in 'like some evil fish', along with the two Smiths and the treasure (93). Like the Islander, so far Small has no redeemable characteristics.

Finally, the writer personifies 'the horrible death' that 'passed so close' to Holmes and Watson 'that night' to emphasise how they flirt with danger. Watson is the more sensitive, as the thought turns him 'sick', while Holmes smiles and shrugs 'his shoulders' (94). This proves how nonchalant Holmes is compared to his sidekick.

Chapter Eleven

In this chapter entitled: 'The Great Agra Treasure' we get the point of view of Small (95). He seems motivated by greed, judging by his 'twinkling eyes' that look 'at the box which had been the cause of his ill-doings' (95). Small admits he 'welted' the Islander 'with the slack end of the rope' for killing Bartholomew, which sounds quite barbaric (95). This was because he 'had no quarrel whatever' with 'this young Sholto' (96).

Meanwhile, Jones is a self-congratulatory mood now that Small is in handcuffs and the case seems to have been resolved. Watson notes that Jones 'was already beginning to give himself airs on the strength of the capture' (97).

When Watson goes to deliver the treasure to Miss Morstan, she appears 'dressed in some sort of white diaphanous material' (98). This makes her seem angelic.

Watson seems impetuous in her presence as he tells her that she and Thaddeus 'will have a couple of hundred thousand each' (99). She seems less than impressed though, as there is 'no eagerness in her voice' (99).

When it turns out that the box is 'empty', Watson can contain himself no longer. He explains his joy to Miss Morstan when he says: 'You are within my reach again' (100). He ends the chapter by saying that he 'gained' 'a treasure' as Mary Morstan reciprocates his love.

Chapter Twelve

Another embedded narrative is about to add a touch more realism to the novel, as the chapter title suggests we will discover 'The Strange Story of Jonathan Small' (101).

Small is still a less than sympathetic character, as he is portrayed leaning 'back in his chair' and laughing 'aloud' when Watson shows him the empty box (101). At this stage, the reader may feel that Miss Morstan has been deprived of the treasure that is rightly hers by a depraved criminal.

Apparently, according to Small, the treasure has been 'scattered' in the river (102). Once he drops 'his mask of stoicism', the reader has a chance to find out what has motivated Small to commit these criminal acts (103).

Through his embedded narrative, Small takes the reader back in time to 1857 and the start of the Indian Rebellion, which he calls 'the great mutiny' (104). He had joined the 'Third Buffs', an army regiment on active service in

India (103). He calls it a time of 'perfect hell', with 'two hundred thousand black devils let loose' (104). Clearly, for today's reader this language sounds incredibly racist, but even Victorian readers would have had little sympathy for this character, albeit for different reasons.

Small seems to think that the indigenous people of India are inferior, as he describes the country as being 'up like a swarm of bees' (105). Bu comparing them to 'bees' and by using the word 'swarm', Small dehumanises the Indian rebels, making them sound like insects.

The word 'swarming' is used by Small to describe 'the city of Agra', which again suggests that the inhabitants are less than human (106). However, he clearly has a higher regard for his 'Punjabees', whom he describes as 'tall, fierce-looking chaps, Mahomet Singh and Abdullah Khan' (107).

These two 'Sikhs' attack him when he lays his 'musket down to strike a match' and hold him at knife-point and gun-point (108). They tell Small that he must chose to join them or die. Small agrees to join them as long as it is not 'against the safety of the fort' (109). Luckily for him, they want him to help them to secure some 'loot' (109). There seems to be honour amongst thieves, as they swear that the treasure must be 'equally divided among the four' of them (109). The additional person involved is 'Dost Akbar', whom Small has not yet met (109).

Singh and Khan tell Small the story of the 'rajah' and his hoarding of 'gold' (109, 110). They are unhappy with the rajah's unwillingness to take sides in the Indian Rebellion, so are resolved to rob him. The rajah has appointed his 'trusty servant', 'Achmet' to look after the rajah's treasure and to deposit it safely in the fort (110). Khan tells Small that his 'foster-brother Dost Akbar' will lead Achmet 'to a side-postern of the fort' where Singh and Khan will lie in wait (110).

Small says that Achmet's life 'was a thing as light as air' to him (110, 111). Once again, this shows him to be an unrepentant murderer. The reader is unlikely to have any sympathy with such a character.

Through pathetic fallacy, the narrative suggests the enormity of the crime about to take place. Small reveals that 'the rain was falling steadily', indicating that something awful is about to happen (111).

Small describes Achmet as 'a little fat, round fellow', who 'seemed to be all in a quiver with fear' (112). It seems even more merciless and cold-blooded to kill such a weak and helpless man. Even Small admits that 'the more' he 'looked at his fat, frightened face, the harder did it seem that we should slay him in cold blood' (113). However, the thought just makes him want 'to get it over' (113). When Achmet tries to escape, Small trips him and Akbar plunges a 'knife twice in his side' (113).

What perturbs Watson most is the 'flippant and careless way' that Small is narrating his story. The reader is reminded once again, that the crimes Small has committed are heinous (114). The moral seems to be that greed can lead to crime.

We return to Small's narrative, as he explains how they cover Achmet's body 'with loose bricks', which is anything but a decent burial (114). Then the criminals make 'a hollow' in the same hall to put their treasure in (115). They are taking much more care of that than they are with the remains of a human being, who has done nothing wrong.

There is some justice, as the four conspirators are 'arrested as the murderers of Achmet' at the end of the Indian Rebellion (116). However, 'not a word about the jewels came out at the trial, for the rajah had been deposed and driven out of India' (116). Hence, the treasure still has not been recovered by the authorities, who are unaware of its existence.

Small bides his time as a prisoner and is eventually relocated to 'Blair Island in the Andamans' (117). While there, he talks to Major Sholto, who is 'a ruined man' following some heavy losses while playing cards (118). Small asks Sholto whether handing over the 'hidden treasure' will get his 'sentence shortened' (118).

Sholto brings Captain Morstan to Small and asks him to repeat the story. Sholto decides it is 'a private concern' rather than a governmental matter (119) and agrees that he and the captain should share a fifth of the treasure, which comes 'to fifty thousand apiece' (120).

Once Small gives Sholto and Morstan the maps, the Major goes off 'to India but' never comes 'back again' (121). Although it's a case of the pot calling the kettle black, Small calls Sholto a 'villain' (121).

Thereafter, Small is completely consumed with thoughts of vengeance as he admits that 'even the Agra treasure had come to be a smaller thing' in his mind compared to 'the slaying of Sholto' (122).

Around that time, Small befriends a 'little Andaman Islander', who is 'sick to death', called 'Tonga' (122). Small nurses Tonga back to health, who ferries him away from the island.

Once Small returns to England with Tonga, he makes 'friends with someone who' can help him (123). He won't 'name no names', so this part of the account remains a mystery, allowing the reader to guess (123).

Alluding to the infamous Victorian freak shows, Small reveals that he profited from 'exhibiting poor Tonga at fair and other such places as the black cannibal' (124). This shows that Small is no stranger to exploiting others for his own gain.

Small describes Tonga 'as proud as a peacock', after the murder of Bartholomew (124). This suggests again, that he sees the Islander as little more than a crude animal. He goes on to describe him as 'a bloodthirsty little imp', which again reveals how little regard he has for him (125).

After Small finishes his story and heads for prison, Watson reveals his engagement to Miss

Morstan. Holmes gives out 'a most dismal groan', which shows how selfish he is (126). Holmes says: 'I really cannot congratulate you' (126). He explains to Watson that 'whatever is emotional is opposed to that true cold reason' which he places above all things (126). Once again, the reader is reminded to align reason with Holmes and emotion with Watson.

The end of the story sees Holmes return to his drug of choice, cocaine. However, before he does that he surmises that Small's 'confederate in the house' was probably Lal Rao and, thinking of himself, quotes Goethe (127). The translation of the quotation is: 'Nature, alas, made only one being out of you although there was material for a good man and a rogue'. These words sum up Holmes's 'Jeckyl and Hyde' nature and indicate he could have ended up as a devious criminal had he not become a detective instead.

Essay writing tips

<u>Use a variety of connectives</u>

Have a look of this list of connectives. Which of these would you choose to use?

'ADDING' DISCOURSE MARKERS

- AND

- ALSO

- AS WELL AS

- MOREOVER

- TOO

- FURTHERMORE

- ADDITIONALLY

I hope you chose 'additionally', 'furthermore' and 'moreover'. Don't be afraid to use the lesser discourse markers, as they are also useful. Just avoid using those ones over and over again. I've seen essays from Key Stage 4 students that use the same discourse marker for the opening sentence of each paragraph! Needless to say, those essays didn't get great marks!

Okay, here are some more connectives for you to look at. Select the best ones.

'SEQUENCING' DISCOURSE MARKERS

- NEXT

- FIRSTLY

- SECONDLY

- THIRDLY

- FINALLY

- MEANWHILE

- AFTER

- THEN

- SUBSEQUENTLY

This time, I hope you chose 'subsequently' and 'meanwhile'.

Here are some more connectives for you to 'grade'!

'ILLUSTRATING / EXEMPLIFYING' DISCOURSE MARKERS

- FOR EXAMPLE

- SUCH AS

- FOR INSTANCE

- IN THE CASE OF

- AS REVEALED BY

- ILLUSTRATED BY

I'd probably go for 'illustrated by' or even 'as exemplified by' (which is not in the list!). Please feel free to add your own examples to the lists. Strong connectives impress examiners. Don't forget it! That's why I want you to look at some more.

'CAUSE & EFFECT' DISCOURSE MARKERS

- BECAUSE

- SO

- THEREFORE

- THUS

- CONSEQUENTLY

- HENCE

I'm going for 'consequently' this time. How about you? What about the next batch?

'COMPARING' DISCOURSE MARKERS

- SIMILARLY

- LIKEWISE

- AS WITH

- LIKE

- EQUALLY

- IN THE SAME WAY

I'd choose 'similarly' this time. Still some more to go.

'QUALIFYING' DISCOURSE MARKERS

- BUT

- HOWEVER

- WHILE

- ALTHOUGH

- UNLESS

- EXCEPT

- APART FROM

- AS LONG AS

It's 'however' for me!

'CONTRASTING' DISCOURSE MARKERS

- WHEREAS

- INSTEAD OF

- ALTERNATIVELY

- OTHERWISE

- UNLIKE

- ON THE OTHER HAND

- CONVERSELY

I'll take 'conversely' or 'alternatively' this time.

'EMPHASISING' DISCOURSE MARKERS

- ABOVE ALL

- IN PARTICULAR

- ESPECIALLY

- SIGNIFICANTLY

- INDEED

- NOTABLY

You can breathe a sigh of relief now! It's over! No more connectives. However, now I want to put our new found skills to use in our essays.

Useful information/Glossary

Allegory: extended metaphor, like the grim reaper representing death, e.g. Scrooge symbolizing capitalism.

Alliteration: same consonant sound repeating, e.g. 'She sells sea shells'.

Allusion: reference to another text/person/place/event.

Ascending tricolon: sentence with three parts, each increasing in power, e.g. 'ringing, drumming, shouting'.

Aside: character speaking so some characters cannot hear what is being said. Sometimes, an aside is directly to the audience. It's a dramatic technique which reveals the character's inner thoughts and feelings.

Assonance: same vowel sounds repeating, e.g. 'Oh no, won't Joe go?'

Bathos: abrupt change from sublime to ridiculous for humorous effect.

Blank verse: lines of unrhymed iambic pentameter.

Compressed time: when the narrative is fast-forwarding through the action.

Descending tricolon: sentence with three parts, each decreasing in power, e.g. 'shouting, talking, whispering'.

Denouement: tying up loose ends, the resolution.

Diction: choice of words or vocabulary.

Didactic: used to describe literature designed to inform, instruct or pass on a moral message.

Dilated time: opposite compressed time, here the narrative is in slow motion.

Direct address: second person narrative, predominantly using the personal pronoun 'you'.

Dramatic action verb: manifests itself in physical action, e.g. I punched him in the face.

Dramatic irony: audience knows something that the character is unaware of.

Ellipsis: leaving out part of the story and allowing the reader to fill in the narrative gap.

End-stopped lines: poetic lines that end with punctuation.

Epistolary: letter or correspondence-driven narrative.

Flashback/Analepsis: going back in time to the past, interrupting the chronological sequence.

Flashforward/Prolepsis: going forward in time to the future, interrupting the chronological sequence.

Foreshadowing/Adumbrating: suggestion of plot developments that will occur later in the narrative.

Gothic: another strand of Romanticism, typically with a wild setting, a sensitive heroine, an older man with a 'piercing gaze', discontinuous structure, doppelgangers, guilt and the 'unspeakable' (according to Eve Kosofsky Sedgwick).

Hamartia: character flaw, leading to that character's downfall.

Hyperbole: exaggeration for effect.

Iambic pentameter: a line of ten syllables beginning with a lighter stress alternating with a heavier stress in its perfect form, which sounds like a heartbeat. The stress falls on the even syllables, numbers: 2, 4, 6, 8 and 10, e.g. 'When now I think you can behold such sights'.

Intertextuality: links to other literary texts.

Irony: amusing or cruel reversal of expected outcome or words meaning the opposite to their literal meaning.

Metafiction/Romantic irony: self-conscious exposure of the devices used to create 'the truth' within a work of fiction.

Motif: recurring image use of language or idea that connects the narrative together and creates a theme or mood, e.g. 'green light' in *The Great Gatsby*.

Oxymoron: contradictory terms combined, e.g. deafening silence.

Pastiche: imitation of another's work.

Pathetic fallacy: a form of personification whereby inanimate objects show human attributes, e.g. 'the sea smiled benignly'. The originator of the term, John Ruskin in 1856, used 'the cruel, crawling foam', from Kingsley's *The Sands of Dee*, as an example to clarify what he meant by the 'morbid' nature of pathetic fallacy.

Personification: concrete or abstract object made human, often simply achieved by using a capital letter or a personal pronoun, e.g. 'Nature', or describing a ship as 'she'.

Pun/Double entendre: a word with a double meaning, usually employed in witty wordplay but not always.

Retrospective: account of events after they have occurred.

Romanticism: genre celebrating the power of imagination, spriritualism and nature.

Semantic/lexical field: related words about a single concept, e.g. king, queen and prince are all concerned with royalty.

Soliloquy: character thinks aloud, but is not heard by other characters (unlike in a monologue) giving the audience access to inner thoughts and feelings.

Style: choice of language, form and structure, and effects produced.

Synecdoche: one part of something referring to the whole, e.g. Carker's teeth represent him in *Dombey and Son*.

Syntax: the way words and sentences are placed together.

Tetracolon climax: sentence with four parts, culminating with the last part, e.g. 'I have nothing to offer but blood, toil, tears, and sweat ' (Winston Churchill).

ABOUT THE AUTHOR

Joe Broadfoot is a secondary school teacher of English and a soccer journalist, who also writes fiction and literary criticism. His former experiences as a DJ took him to far-flung places such as Tokyo, Kobe, Beijing, Hong Kong, Jakarta, Cairo, Dubai, Cannes, Oslo, Bergen and Bodo. He is now PGCE and CELTA-qualified with QTS, a first-class honours degree in Literature and an MA in Victorian Studies (majoring in Charles Dickens). Drama is close to his heart as he acted in 'Macbeth' and 'A Midsummer Night's Dream' at the Royal Northern College of Music in Manchester. More recently, he has been teaching 'A' Level and GCSE English Literature and IGCSE and GCSE English Language to students at secondary schools in Buckinghamshire, Kent and in south and west London.